## THE BASKET-MAKER'S RHYME

*I can rand,*
*At your command,*
*Put on a decent border;*
*Upset tight,*
*Wale all right,*
*And keep my stakes in order.*

# CANEWORK

## CHARLES CRAMPTON

With an Introduction to the History
of Basket-making and some Notes on
Cane and Its Uses by H. H. Peach

## THE DRYAD PRESS
### LEICESTER

*Twelfth Edition*    1951

*Published by the Dryad Press*
*Printed in Great Britain at*
*The Curwen Press Ltd., Plaistow*

# CONTENTS

Fig. 4. CORACLES AFLOAT. NETTING FOR SALMON

Fig. 5. EXAMPLES OF POTTERY, SHOWING IMPRESSION OF
RUSH MAT ON WHICH THE POT WAS FORMED. FROM
AMORGOS. BRONZE AGE
IMPRESSION OF SLATH BOTTOM OF BASKET SHOWN ON BASE
OF POT FROM PHYLAKOPI, MELOS. DATE *c*. 2500 B.C.
*Examples in Ashmolean Museum, Oxford. Reproduced by permission.*

of the basket upon my head '. Coiled baskets of this sort are used in Egypt and Palestine to this day and carried on the head.

Mr. C. T. Woolley found impressions of coiled basket-work on pottery at Ur in Mesopotamia about 3000 B.C. Herodotus, in the fifth century B.C., tells of basket boats covered with bitumen being used on the Euphrates, and such boats are still used there to-day, also in India. The skin-covered coracle of our forefathers can still be seen on the Severn.

It seems probable that the peoples of Northern Europe made a type of basket-work starting with the slath base and not coiled work, owing to the use of willow. The slath does not seem to occur in ancient Egyptian work. The furthest south where examples have been found of this till after Roman times, is in the Greek island of Melos, where a piece of pottery has been found made by a Northern race, on which the impression of the slath is to be seen. An example is in the Taylorian Museum in Oxford, the date being about 2500 B.C. They also have a piece with the impression of a rush basket, suggesting in both cases that the basket was used as mould for the pottery.

Baskets were connected with both Greek and Roman religious life, where they were the receptacle for the offerings to the gods. Likewise in Christian times we find a symbol of the eucharist — the loaves and fishes—includes a basket as a receptacle.

The Romans made furniture of wicker, and Pliny tells us that they and the Etruscans reclined upon couches of willow.

The example of a Roman wicker chair given in Fig. 6 is from a tombstone in the Treves Museum, and the type of gravestone can be seen repeated in coarser workmanship in the Mainz Museum, etc.

The English tradition in basket-work is inherited from the Celts, and Fig. 7 shows a very early British example of what was probably a wattle wall. Several Roman writers refer to the prevalence of this method of hut building in Great Britain.

It is possible that the excellent willows grown in northern Europe influenced the type of basket made, just as one finds in Norway and Sweden the split wood basket, which still exists in the Lake District and at Bewdley. The swills, as they are called

Fig. 6. ROMAN WICKER CHAIR, *c.* A.D. 200, TREVES

Fig. 7. SPECIMEN OF BASKET-WORK FOUND IN GLASTONBURY
LAKE VILLAGE EXCAVATIONS; EARLY IRON AGE

*By kind permission of Dr. A. Bulleid, F.S.A., and Mr. H. St. George Gray, F.S.A.*

*Chinese Baskets*, by Berthold Laufer, Curator of Anthropology. (Field Museum of Natural History, Chicago.)

*Some Technological Notes from the Pomeroon District, British Guiana*, by Dr. Walter E. Roth. Part III. (Royal Anthropological Institute of Great Britain and Ireland, London.)

'Some Commercial Notes on Baskets', by Hugo H. Miller. (Page 485 of *The Philippine Craftsman*, January 1914. Published by Bureau of Education, Manila.)

## CANE AND ITS GROWTH

British Empire Exhibition, Rattan Malayan Records, XVII.

*Common Products of India*, by Sir G. Watt. (Murray, 1908.)

*A Manual of Indian Timbers*, by J. S. Gamble. 2nd edition. (Sampson Low, 1922.) Gives list of canes, p. 734.

Kew Bulletin, 1899, p. 200.

Malayan Forest Records, No. 2, 1922.

*De Nuttige Planten van Nederlandsch-Indie*, by K. Heyne. Part I. Batavia, 1911.

Agricultural Bulletin of the Straits and Federated Malay States, No. 2, by H. N. Ridley. (Singapore, 1903.) Pp. 129–136, 159–160.

## WILLOW AND ITS GROWTH

A Monograph of the British Willows, by Rev. E. F. Linton, M.A. (West, Newman & Co., 1913.)

*Cultivation of Osiers and Willows*, by Wm. Paulgrave Ellmore. (Dent, 1919.)

*Cultivation of Osiers and Willows*. Board of Agriculture and Fisheries Miscellaneous Publications, No. 18. (H.M. Stationery Office, 1913.)

*Korbweidenbau*, by von Wissmann. (Deutsche Landwirtschafts-Gesells., Berlin, 1928.)

*Korbweidenbau und Bandstockbetriebe*, by E. Kern. (Oberleutnant Kern, Osnabruck, 1904.)

*Osiériculture*, by E. Leroux. (Librairie J.-B. Baillière, Paris, 1921.)

*The Rural Industries of England and Wales*. 4 vols. See Vol. I and Vol. IV. (Oxford Press.)      H. H. Peach

## Twin Basket.

No. 12 cane   30" long     Protrude 5"
below base — nail canes to base
Work 2 rows of 3rds upsetting above
base, end below base before
foot track   No. 9 cane.

  Landing for 3-4 rows
Byelaw of No. 12.

  row of Waling occasionally to break
monotony.   2" — 11½" — 5½"